NIGHT
FIELD
ANECDOTE

NIGHT
FIELD
ANECDOTE

POEMS

WILLIAM WRIGHT

Louisiana Literature Press
Hammond, Louisiana

Printed in the United States of America

FIRST EDITION, 2011

Cover Design: Chad Pelton, 2011

Author's Photo: Sandra DuTeau, 2009

Requests for Permission to reproduce material from this work should be sent to:

Louisiana Literature Press

SLU Box 10792

Hammond, LA 70402

ISBN: 978-0-945083-32-0

Library of Congress Cataloging-in-Publication Data

Wright, William, 1979-
  Night field anecdote : poems / William Wright. ~ 1st ed.
     p. cm.
  I. Title.
  PS3623.R59N54 2011
  811'.6~dc23
                                        2011035659

Acknowledgments

Thanks to the editors of the journals in which the following poems appeared or will soon appear, sometimes with different titles and in slightly different forms:

Agni: "Chernobyl Eclogue"

Beloit Poetry Journal: "Peach Trees, Suffused with Pesticides"

Birmingham Poetry Review: "Blond Mare, Iredell Co., NC, 1870-1896," "Prayer to Worms"

Colorado Review: "Blue Pear"

Comstock Review: "In Defiance of Autumn," "The Tide," "The Burden"

Connecticut Review: "Teleology: Recurring Dream," "Creature Comfort," "Snake Lore"

Devil's Lake: "Wolf Spider"

Epoch: "White Fox"

Floyd County Moonshine: "The Potato"

Grist: "Trumpet Creeper" (sections two and three), "Ghost Water," "Bluebird"

Indiana Review: "Hell"

Louisiana Literature: "The Other Body," "Spirits of Old Mountain Road"

Midwest Quarterly: "Winter Oaks"

New Orleans Review: "Prescribed Fire"

New South: "The Escape"

North American Review: "Trumpet Creeper" (section one)

Poetry South: "Trumpet Creeper" (all sections), "Nightmares for the Seasons"

Shenandoah: "Equus," "Family Portrait, 1790"

Smartish Pace: "Burning House," "Nocturne for the Second Death"

Southern Poetry Review: "Ferns," "Loggerhead Shrike," "Sweet Gums near Pond at Night"

Spoon River Poetry Review: "Eclogue: Drowning"

Tar River Poetry: "Rabid Cat"

Texas Review: "Bledsoe," "Before Dawn," "Gravity"

Valley Voices: "Strays"

For Michelle

Contents

I

FECUNDITY

Sweet Gums near Pond at Night

1.

Summer hauls away
its load
of storms, having dragged
its name again
through the gossip
of sudden rains.

I am still,
sleepless, afraid to move,
as though what keeps me
awake breathes this solemn room
alive, grinning behind me
in the hackled dark.

As though a couple
gazes in through the window,
my insomnia the final answer
to their longing
for the afterlife, voices
flickering blue
in their open mouths.

2.

Now I can hear
the tall, sullen heads
of the sweet gums outside

lean into one another,
unlatching autumn
from its deep hiding.

The pond knows
to keep silent,
showing the world only itself,
its mouth full
of secrets closed.

3.

I want to lie down and rest, embroidered
into autumn's declension,
recalling nothing, no voice,

to know the blood
of the earth rushes over my skull
and trust it is music.

Trumpet Creeper

1.

June light comes again
and again without remorse:
Pollen rummages the scalps
of spent deciduous hour after hour
until two sycamores puffed open by the wind bend
over the creek in twin green flames. Lacertilian armies
raze the garden and the yard's fringes,
flares for ruby-throats, bees.

Around the bowed trunks the loam shoots forth
lush feelers, sprung broad then clustered,
pink star-trails drooped at the stalk
and bursting
now to hum a song I almost hear.

*

Coiled red mouths, they bloom beyond the shed
into unhinged greenness,
brighten, pump, swell through everything,
fall flaccid,
foiling their own morphology.

All spines suffer their histories, blossom-lattices
formed from water
in microfossil plumes,
when great black smokers

billowed up, kelp-like shifts,
fields of ducts, white worms, smokestacks—
a trillion trillion cellular divinities.

Preglacial, they shift into woods and out again,
coil and articulate
deciduous nooks, flaunt the seasonal genesis:
vast gasps of light and air,
power of galaxies held forever in the lungs.

*

After June rain, I turn my back to the animals, the hush-
hush metaphors, abandon a green too brilliant
and face the black interstices of the tree-wall.

I feel the imminent collapse, the mass,
vibrissa crowding the ribcage,
my skeleton tranformed under
the leaf-kiss, deep earth
watered down,
gourd unwrapped like a gift.

*

Heaven is neither lamb nor lion: Heaven
is symmetry's absence,
a trumpet creeper's seedpod
drained down the dead man's throat.

Strands and stalks expand
beyond order, uncontainable,
pierce thistle and stone:

Whittled to hair and bone,
the beast rolls its leaf-lobed head,
howls new identities.

2.

Summer sky an old onion.
Over the fence flares of pink trumpets.
Bees wheel about their coral bells, fly off.

*

I am meat, salt, water.
In my skull hums
a three pound sentient chunk.
When I kiss my mother's hair,
a sleeping giant's heart blooms, collapses.

He shifts in his sleep and smiles,
mica flashing.

One day he'll look me in the eye.

*

A fleet of cumuli leans away.
Freighted with rain, bees drop
to the freshened grass,
red clover.

3.

My great uncle Basil died when he was five years old
on a farmhouse floor in Iredell County, North Carolina,
half his face boiled from his skull.

Quilts and winter storms
broke my great-grandmother
to bone and a scorched gown,

pre-dawn dimness on a copper cauldron
that held the lye he tipped and spilled,
his little fingers charred,
hard as rust.

*

Sleeves of corn stalks flapped and clattered,
ash in the chimney flue, plum jelly's bright jar.

My grandfather turned in
his mother's darkness, eyes fusing.

*

As the calyx
unsheathes a petal,

as the hand holds
the scalded hand,

furled leaf,
heat to breathe and bear.

As water scars deep grain,
cottonmouths uncurl

over roots that twine kin
to smilax and larkspur:

the stream's clear coil.

Burning House

Even though you only remember a pewter spoon,
the sap-dark core of oak and your mother's
long shadow snapping the screen door,

the ax strikes the wood's black heart:
You haul and stack racks of ruined cedar, ember
of the kitchen window across the blackberry and ice,

suffer the fox hour down the hill to suppers
of hot cabbage with salt and water, parsley and rye—
Even when the house smolders, crossbeams

hissing and finding their own charred context,
you step into the May-rush of another fire,
another room that spins and seethes.

The whole field, a sleeve of smoke.
Behind the wall, vermiculate hands,
the dark spring river.

Blonde Mare, Iredell County, NC, 1870 – 1896

No one thinks of you anymore, your bones now broken
beneath the barn's dark rutted boards, turning
with coal, grass, and stars, those few deathless sovereigns.

Who witnessed you blossoming from the stable's
downslant of light, those mounds of golden hay
and chaff your grainy world until the fields lay open?

They worked you hard, your muscles hauling Scots plow
through furrow, chisel and coulter loosening earth
till dusk. They'd prod you and you'd chuff.

But now they are with you, too, all knitted by death's
twine, your crux not lost but heaved by creek
and meadow, sluiced through the blowing manes of trees.

Equus

Dusks a blue smolder of memory:
Your grandfather fades behind the creak
of the barn door, mouth trembling with sermons
lodged forever behind his tongue. You breathe

dust and drink the well's rust-water,
then slog in the heat of horses,
saddled by noon rains, mud choking the yield.
Nights, back in the stanch purity of those rooms,

with soap-burned hands you wrap your head
with words: sorghum and lantern, cellar and sin.
Then down into image, the earth's nightlong gift:
Your mother's scarred hands fondling the plump coinage

of tomatoes, the pox of aphids washed immaculate.
Her gloves uncoiling barbed wire, gauzing the reddening scrape.
The hiss and warmth of embers, cedar-smoke's tang.
Always she dims again beneath black water

as mornings wrest you from sleep like a breech foal
torn loose, shivering in the hay.

Snake Lore

They would thrash and hiss
in my great-grandmother's tales—
a rattler, hours after
its head was severed
by her axe, that bit her dog;
or the moccasin, frozen stick-stiff
and brought in to thaw
that sang in two voices:
one low growl that rattled
the floorboards, one high
melody in an unknown tongue.

She told of a young girl's autumn
picking apples and pears
under moon-sign: The woods smelled
of bread and rotting poplar,
the thick musk of hidden snakes.
The last night of harvest she dreamed
orchards bursting with the dusk-hued fruit
of serpents, a leathery sky bending
to the colorless, farsighted morning
she woke to, the day's drudgery
locked in her bones.

Rolling pit-vipers
over her knuckles like oil
in those raucous mountain chapels,
chanting in the sway of bodies
and tongues striking the bright air,

she guessed the brains
in those pineal heads
held knowledge more luminous
than even the faithful could conjure
in their mortal, seasonal skin.

Prayer to Worms

Dear annelid dark, forgive us
our soil, stabbed through with silicate
and diatom, the sudden river that mocks

your movement through fields.
Forgive us the birds, those sickles of sky
that sweep you up for the gagging throats

of their young. Absolve us of our searing
roads that bake you hard and gray,
summer's tiny slaughter.

You weave your silent thunder through
the dark, you imply: *The sky is a god
long dead* as you bind down into igneous origins,

ancient loam that loves you,
soon stalled in the sun-struck orchards
where blooms again the vital leaf.

The Potato

I wanted to be a potato, all brain and eyes,
born into the rhythm of worms, roots' suck
that throbbed me to life. When the field leaned

into fall, before the first frost reconfigured the sun,
I'd tremble in the hum of the hill's vegetable dark.
Sight clogged by loam, my nature saved from gravity,

I'd confound the apple, which drops abruptly
forever, bruised by limbs, the windfall flesh
sloughed into the yellow grass of my many throats.

I'd turn in a womb-furrow, a planetoid unhinged
from orbit. Above me a thick door would unbolt.
Plumped, warmed by the sun's annunciation,

I'd submit to the hunger of anyone who knocked
the earthen garments from my body, lifted me to air.

Bluebird

Morning's windfall light flecks this chapel of bone.
Houseflies drone, scatter alms, minor chords
strummed in stained grass:

Up close the inside becomes Byzantine,
a palm-sized vault, ribs rows of pews.

Out of the body burst ants and their sanctity
to clip the plum lungs

and heart,
bear the flesh home.

Before Dawn

You'll have to understand the earth
as you sleep, how somewhere

below the floorboards' wheezes
and groans, below

the leaf mold and fibrous shelves
expanding in cellar air,

under the root-clogged dirt sluiced
with caves of bone,

hair and blood, the dead speak
their own language.

You discern loam and star—no matter
how singular your focus,

their words muddle in your blood's
own susurrant force,

your ear an oar heaving toward birdsong
and the day's first wind

ceding to sun, morning's
loyal erasure.

Teleology: Recurring Dream

1.

If the door opens into an oak grove,
an intense greenness sentient with sun

and wind, avoid predication: with your eyes
masked by your hands,

say: *Our brains are lanterns*
on this dark river.

2.

If you venture into the cold smell
of stone, recent rain on slate,

or witness spars of elderberry
and jasmine's parched umbilicus,

admit: *The moon is a requiem,*
its bone-pile light another entrance.

3.

What you carry, carry.
Put down what you put down.

If you fail to close the door behind you,
how will you acknowledge the world

without distraction? How will you
know that, even in dead

silence, a sound hums the cells?

Ferns

Hard to trust the way they spin and nod in the light,
always looking away.

Older than the creeks they flank, their fossil tongues
fold to the sun in green, outstretched

syllables, asking their one question. When a body passes,
they turn and glare, eyes nested deep

in their black heads. Dense and sentient with more
history than the sweet gum that seeps

and falls, or ground water that diminishes
in the fattening sun, these reversed medusas

lick through stone, outstare all the locked houses
of blood and hair, outspeak

the millennial sky-clatter of bird language, leaf-litter
and lichen, reach out, take.

Prescribed Fire

Rain stirs clover and rot, rouses the beehive's thrum,
barn slats tiered in fungus. From bloodroot to cinder,
leaf-mold and cedar smoke bitter in six weeks' deepness.
Autumn deserves nothing it demands,
not ghost or doxology:

Say *soon cinnamon and cider, soon scuppernong and gourd.*
Years from now, the body disassembles; bees drowse
in their cells. Ash drifts through the field's red sumac,
spectral edge where two hounds guard
bright scraps of their kill.

No matter: A word rises the moment it is spoken.
Past fodder stacks and tobacco, near the small
blue vase on the sill, garlic crackles
and pales in a broth near-boil,
rain quells and the heart
owns its one room.

Family Portrait, 1790

North Carolina Blue Ridge

Here earth juts and tumbles in woods
where mountain creeks purl, slake through
rock, sluice schist coves and sheltered

gaps, then push hard through piebald sheer,
down to the slant of a cabin leaning:
Dusk's long shadow flickers dark

in this singular room, where my kin huddle
around bacon and cabbage that snaps,
burbles over pine-hiss and ember—

Fire grinds the weight of nightfall
on their silence, toil-dark scowls
over tight frowns, throats hungry

to down day's reaping. Here, land
is the sole tongue, etched in intricate syntax
of apple and trillium, the garden's blood-idiom,

husk-dry stanzas quenched by prophecies
of rain. Nights, when their worn out bodies
die into sleep, their dreams ration

to applewood and rattlers, valleys' tobacco
and fodders stacks, the few words passed
down that I take with me, write down, and move on.

Spirits of Old Mountain Road

My grandfather warned me that ghosts lurked
outside his house, even in winter, ate clay
and summoned storms. Denouncing heaven,
they were born again from the deepest heartwood

of oaks and elms, he claimed, their wet-sleek bodies
hatched from the trees' wombs in the dead of spring,
when limbs unlocked green fires: They came back to declare
things lost or forgotten, the barn's flagrant red,

jars of pig's feet, a blunted ax left to rain.
Summers we'd walk and cock our heads,
listen until certain fields deafened, crickets
sawing a static that crackled utterance,

shunted down the valley's ragged vein.
That's the way they talk, he'd whisper. *And their throats open
in them berms yonder.* Those hills, lined with plush
syllables of plum and apple, sated

until stars reminded us to turn back:
In last light, mosquitoes piercing
my aching legs alive, we returned to his farm's
dim ember in the horizon's dark, drunk

on the hymns of those unseen kin, drunk
on the balm of that land's green language.

Creature Comfort

Even if loneliness sits on your eyelids nightly,
a skin of white fields and stone
skies your body refuses to shed—

know at least that the earth will remember
you, as you remember the corn snake
under your father's porch years ago,

how it curled up in the rotten wood
and dandelion like a red and white ribbon.
For days it lay motionless, the sun-glint

proving its eyes unendurably clear and alive,
the heat in that light keeping it still.
Know at least that one night, the grass bowed

as the snake slackened loose the crisp ghost
of itself, uncoiled its torsional radiance
and passed into the dark.

II

Ruin

Bledsoe

1.

Behind the brick pits
    of Saluda County Waterworks,

Durant Bledsoe wobbles
    out of the sumac and bellwort,

grimaces pink-skinned
    at how the world spins, swings

to the right. Hobbles along
    the tree line from the braid

of sirens, the asphalt's linear
    prophecy, his forehead super-

heated and scathed in the sweeping
    back and flay of limbs.

Gasping. Shame a char-smear
    on his ear. (Sweat begins to rinse

that hollowness away.) Hemorrhage-hot,
    dead center, the sun grinds

his muttering down to bear declaration,
    (whine and howl):

Ain't no need to warsh, Mama,
    when I seen your blood the while.

Ain't no need to warsh, Mama
    when you're bald of mouth and eyes.

Smells of smolder, choking
    on panic with trees leaning in.

2.

Time to leave you, boy. I'd suture you to me
    if I could. Closed her eyes: Cancer

crawled in her like spiderlings
    hatching from withered sacs

of her lungs. Walked wincing.
    From her bed the salve-smell

sweat on sheets: always around
    him. The ache, always: She begged

and begged nightly for years—
    Boy, all I ask is a smother

in my sleep. Curl up some hemlock
    in my tea. Out. He needing

out from the blunt weight of her smock
    as she sat at dinner, forking

the bread, eating nothing. *Durant,*
   you ain't got no sense to know I suffer.

You ain't got a mind to do nothing.
   Land's feculence suffocating him

in its shoveled-over residue. Her breath
   like leafmeal, apples set to blister in

the August sear. Take no mind
   of the molder. Turn your head away.

3.

In the keening house, in the night's arc
   over her coughing fits and pleadings,

he stargazes from his pallet.
   A rush of living dark tears through

the country air, through the tall grasses,
   shakes loose over his sternum. To share

the panic of fleeing creatures—
   The awful fact of leaving her

dead and cooling in the house. No matter
   how far his flight, her body would mound

under quilts, her flesh would swell
   blue in the room whorled with stench.

So with the flick of a flame, there it would go.
    Went. Cross-beams seethed and cracked

the end. The farm's old bones unlatched
    a tall blaze, dawn behind a cloud of gasoline.

4.

Dusk comes, heat stays, still
    douses his hair in salt, sweat.

Lost, lulled by dark, Durant misreads
    the far hound's yowl as lullaby.

He limps on down to the stream
    bank, briar lashes needling

chiggers on his skin. Down further
    to the tick-leafed, scallop-prongs

of the sand-slews, rushes and snarl
    of water full of musk-smell,

cottonmouths folding their bodies
    deeper under, spring's bulls

and peepers terror-plopping.
    He washes scalp, face,

blood and cinder away and gone.
    Then, cooled, props his head

against the berm and ponders on
    her teeth, gnashed in

the death-frown, her eyes astonished
    and rolled-back white.

Bites down gently on his tongue,
                      sleeps.

5.

A blackness amplified, greenness insinuated:
    The insects chisel the night to a point, summer

clouds bear no star. Beyond the tangle of limbs
    and detritus of a thousand falls, out east

toward the farms and the clearing, the house
    lies in a pile of smolder. What seeps

into the brain's dark apertures? What ignites
    the night's grammar or douses it silent

(something sheer and simple for once)?—
    Sepal-green, the earth's rejuvenating

pain. Suddenly, a man lies down
    in his guilt and asks: Are you the lattice

or the bloom? Answers come as platitudes,
    tricks of dead light, peripheral. Thus sleep

forces signs, trespass, yellow dust in the throat.
  Summer turns quick yet heavy-footed,

more potent than the fever
  that bleeds through him like a bloom.

6.

Something deep in Durant's vitals
  strikes violent, itch turned pain

turned mania, clot in neck-vein
  and thalamus twinge. Heat holiness.

Body slumps, simply still
  in the climbing scald of morning.

7.

They find him near noon,
  the law's dogs set crazed on his reek.

Even as they haul him away,
  looking for the right cage for him

to wither in, his mind lies
  distant, radiant. Trees flower,

lean away, give him
  room. Eyes scoured, his face

calcified, a coin set gleaming
  in the closing vault of days.

Rabid Cat

Rags of cheek sagged from the jawbone's white.
The sick mouth snarled, pocked throat
frothing half-rattle, half-growl.
When it dragged death's pong along the yard,
my father rigged a trap of chicken, wire,
and a stone meant to break its scabrous back,
which worked: Since madness shook the squirrel heart
in its gut, the gnawed mouth brave
enough to clink the latch trigger.
As if the bludgeon wasn't plenty,
my father aimed the gun and sprayed
the cat red onto the porch-wall.

Into morning, with gloves, bleach, and scalding soap-water,
we crouched into that pale gore, our sinuses torched
raw, hair steam-wilted, scooping jelly viscera into bags.
Pre-dawn lit the bed I'd lie sleepless in, that demon
eyeing my dream's door, and my father, dog-tired,
would heft the skull bits to the trees.

Eclogue: Drowning

This is the time of musk and mint, helix of silver minnows.
This is the dream in which leaves hinder.

Bayberry rushes eye sockets, blooms new answers. If the mouth opens,
taste mulberry and soot. Let the feet sidestep any omen.

Wind unshackles rain, the creek's eelgrass
flat on alabaster, water a long grave.

Small bodies hide: throb of bees behind
barn walls, their hymn

a voice: *You are a green cell curled in an amnion of leaves.*
A voice: *Snakes drag their dark fires beneath the shale.*

When the door's hinge cracks loose, your fingers
disturb the silt. When the silt is disturbed, your hair

becomes the grass's ghost. Lungs pull down
your mouth, your eyes to clay.

You will not see the marks your hands create.
You will not see the fossils your hands become.

Nightmares for the Seasons

1. *Spring*

Pond's bottom: the dead, frayed
meadowlark wavers,
slow in the grammar of gar—

The hollow eye, unfeasibly black,
stares backward through its own bones.

2. *Summer*

Starving, you eat the pale berries,
juice stinging your tongue:

Summer woods lean
in: the sun,

torn gauze uncoiling.

3. *Autumn*

Big as horses, wolves snarl behind you.
Your scent blows back to their snouts,
wild and bloody is the darkening sun.

Wind smells of wood smoke, a fire
on the ridge: Your house.

A wolf has been here where man
or animal lies at road's edge,
eaten in red sumac.

Ribs, out of which the purple vitals
spill where they do not belong.

Far distance:
Cold salt of the night's first stars.

4. *Winter*

Your sentience in another's mouth,
in the voiceless mouth
of a name expunged.

Your utterance frozen
and lodged in the throat,
syllables of cracking boughs
and the ice-scarred leaf.

Fever

1.

You remember that tall Mexican
come out of the orchard
with bloody hands.
Sweat salt on his hat-brim and shirt collar.

Chewed on hard candy that looked like sapphires.
Didn't had but seven teeth.

Raked back a leaf patch: Copperhead snagged
his foot to the hard vein.

2.

All around the trees breathed on
their invisible exchanges, arborescent
heat-shimmer, light-eating leaf.

Foot swollen with venom,
he stumbled into a vision of relics
piled under his mother's bed:

(feather drum, wolf eye):

O madre,
I cup the helix in my hands
and let my faith wash through me.
I am the xylem of the Lord

3.

Engine oil guttation,
leaves greased and sagging in August heat.

Boots streaked with dust.
Head tilted back to nurse his third Sol.

4.

The truth of his delirium: her womb
lopsided with hemorrhage. Her brain the shell of a locust:

Hermana, I have no choice but to burn your little brown house

5.

His sister took the painting of a great storm cloud
raining from its belly a heap of red blooms.

for converting gasoline
to glossolalia, singeing the hair and the gown.

6.

Half-drunk, he ate breakfast at the PK diner.
When they surrounded him, he shook his head,
claiming deafness.

Peach Trees, Suffused with Pesticides

Hummingbirds stop
to bathe in the creases of leaves
where each least grass spider
has left the husk of its body.
The sky ravels in the throat

when ends of limbs tremble, unlatch their petals
to a distant sea of hands:

the body
cannot scrub it out, this lack
of stain, emptiness gathering.

Chernobyl Eclogue

1. *Day*

Guards nod our white van toward Pripyat's yellow prairie, where
refusniks hunker in robin's-egg-blue sheds. Peat-smoke
coughs from chimneys. "That smoke makes
plutonium," I say, and Sasha answers
"*Da*," almost too soft to hear.

Sasha is contaminated. We ride to his district,
tall grasses iridescent, swath of weak sun
peeling more than bark from birch. "It's the little
things," he says, though the forest
that's overtaken the carnival,

bleached of color, first catches my eyes. I know I won't
remember this: It's the sort of forgetfulness
the day demands: Sky's milky iris
dragging the afternoon, light
like a snapped bone.

Strontium roots deeper in his teeth when he speaks.
Licks his lips: "Old mother will say: 'We've survived
two bouts of starvation, and now
something invisible will kill us?
We'll stay here.'"

In the middle distance, her husband steps out from the fence,
his legs wrapped in pig hide below the knees.
He smiles, toothless, and as we close in,
I see the Holsteins, the harnesses.
The man's white eyes.

Inside—mushrooms. The couple has spent the day at harvest,
cooked these brown ribs cored with cesium,
wet with steam. They smell like rye but taste
of the autumn floor, rills spiced
with leaf-mold and rain.

At dusk, my head feels like a gourd in which the day
rattles. The sheds swarm and puddle with laughs,
and a little girl, her shaved head like a stubble
of gray corn, trails her soiled dress
through mud-slick grass.

2. *Night*

Window's rust-light. I won't remember it. Memory
like groundwater radiates to weeds that jag
a shrew's belly, a hill-wolf that keeps its mouth

closed. Distant lumber truck huffs to Belarus.
And these small rooms, hot with stubbornness,
hot with some soft poison that leaks between them.

Sasha lies down next to me, his bare spine blanched
almonds in the moonlight. Behind the paper wall,
the fire snaps its half-life out to new snow.

The Other Body

Fog hovers above water, exact twine
    of the creek made ghost—
Moving like darkness beneath the skin.
    The same dark holds
oil in the leaf that fires silences
      of this autumn day.

Body in health, body in death,
    inscribing its downward
logic, the unfinished phrase:
    capillary's nexus, ellipses

of wing-bone and glacier, a sweetness
    in the milk and whistling
of a honey bee's musculature.
    The body's language

lingers, dissipates, always moving,
    even as the sea stalls
arms and legs to falling: Deep hum of silica
    in oak, the green crush
of vines in sun, blood's thrum
      stilled, spoken for.

The Burden

On that Sunday, when the doctors confirmed the worst,
the slate-light clouds threatened, pounded their walls
of nothingness, hastened to unbolt your nerves
to the bitter poem you could never write.

Afraid, you dreamed fires blooming
in the attic, undetectable and finally encircling,
scorching the world that lay in you. Then,
when the pain seeped in, the wind bent

the branches outside, where you watched that cage
of stars, felt the dead deer's eyes follow you
when you paced. Your irises took the color
of a glacier, persistent, ancient, inevitable.

In your veins they sluiced with medicine, you sensed
ghosts mourn more for themselves than for you.
Not self-pity: Two nights before your death,
you walked in the orchard you loved

and witnessed the mutt circle its clear ache,
collapse in that husk of leafless limbs to assent
to the rain and worm that would reshape
its body for that dark country.

III

AFTERGLOW

Blue Pear

He lies reed-like in his bed as in his mind,
a lure to ghosts and master
of measuring light,

understands how the moon
finds under the elm leaves
just beyond the window

a raccoon's carcass, its mouth
and intestines ulcerated and sloughed
to runnels. A blue pear

lifted from a bowl. Minnows
prodding rain-scalloped shores, each spine
anchored for the moment's purpose.

He knows the elm is a cathedral
through which crows shake
and bend dark rafters,

leaf-light patinas on the far wall.
What is the music that falls on the grass,
retreats into the shuttered dark?

The man singing at the house's far end,
his mind a halved blue pear.

White Fox

She knows the fox's smell: ice and moldering apple,
the smallest contours of his mask—

She discerns the world as a slanted slate of white,
the smallest fracture, movement:

snake's arc in bayberry, the urn of a mouse's bones
picked clean. And as the fields outside

fall upward into snow, she sees how night shackles
her body, bright and plausible,

a mammal warmth, a vase of milk. When she tastes
his breath, all earth and fur,

an orchard afire, she knows the white fox has come
to sleep in the garden of her

mind, now bodiless,
red leaf on stone.

Loggerhead Shrike

Trapped between sleep and wakefulness,
      mind perched in the high rafter, she sees
the shale tuft of its wing flared under the night's
        shimmering arbor, the delicate articulations

of its kill: Out near the pond's muddy mirage,
      the shrike impales its shrew on a barbed-wire fence
and twists, empties that small cup of bones.
      Between earth and star, water and vacuum,

high clouds glow, the world's arc folds distances
      between Asia and her right iris, the eye which won't
close, raveling the dark story her brain demands told—
      night's blue omen a shadow on the wall.

Wolf Spider

Three nights in succession, the earth has pulled dawn
to the chapel, the first light-smear like a thorax split,
blood-arc, sky a spilled wound. Graves shimmer
like quartz on the hill, where loam craves
strong spring rain.

The chapel's windows, toothed and gleaming. No one
knows why the yard's trees hiss hymns. No one knows
how the spiders, deep in hydrangea, seal behind
them calipers of space, stitch gossamer
bloom to bloom.

Thus the heart moves to a warmer room, attuned
to April trees. Thus the bee is caught in clouds
of filament, wrapped, gored, and eaten.
No matter: the leaf still increases
in the eaves.

The storm grows, spiders scatter, and bent grass
acquiesces to summer. When thunder riots
foliage, rattles the panes, holy relics gleam
blue on the altar. The night will always
swagger forth and fall.

Nocturne for the Second Death

At first, the wind sustains us, holds us aloft like gossamer:
the first sting of snow blown off dwarf pine
into towns that still constellate their fires,
dream and hoard the dimming myths.

To know the earth, we record expanse: meadow's longitude,
river-crux and the salt-sick coast. We search
farms of blighted corn, lean with their husks
to hear underground streams snap

and sluice dry roots into the running. To know the earth,
we record microcosm: pine needle and paramecium,
pumpkin seeds rotting in hay. Always, when moths
raid the ruined factory and chew gowns to powder,
thronging the air with larvae,

one of us will stray: because the ice in her mouth is a lily
opening, because he leaves the purity of hunger
in a starved fox's belly, lets maggots eat the gray eyes
to a dark scald. But we are forever assimilable,
even when the lights of the earth's curve

lock all the doors: We will wait centuries for the youngest
to boast and swagger in the silence he has become,
to stitch the sky as if he could bolster the light.
He returns as the last ember's hiss,
the last frost unsheathed.

Even spring, buried in water, we keep ourselves
down with the briar and bramble. When we can't bear to be
forgotten anymore, not by sludge or sleet, we unload
the bright syllables of our hair and skin,
then move on, torches in a tomb.

The Escape

We take to the burning farms,
   bent forward and quick through chaff:
      our mother gone to gossip of the eastern bay,
         her hair sewn with gray leaves of that place.

Father stays behind, hauling
   wood from the land's silver scar,
      his strength perfunctory in the rain.
         Towns of torn roofs, torn mouths:

Church bells toll wide vowels
   through grass, the path to the other world.
      When country roads, farms and houses
         reflect just enough light

to state the dark, we assemble on the hill,
   windows of our hands letting matter pass
      through, cartilaginous tulip bulbs,
         primed to fill the spring's maw.

Field wolves snarl loose the hearts
   of slow cattle, snouts bloody in the starlight:
      We pass the slate of their eyes.
         Rustle and grain, rustle and char,
            our footprints already in front of us.

Tap Water

Without moving, the pipes contain
phrases, a dream-language

she can't evade, even when the moon
slants in, bathes her face

of any discernable fear: Thus her eyes
move in the knowledge

that underground, someone sits up
in the wolf-eyed dark, counting

with a voice of water, charting
how her body, stilled as it is,

writhes against those lucid syllables,
defies the blindness of that prophecy.

Ghost Water

We enter the pond during a night of glassy corners:
Frost toughens the grass, slows red oaks
until leaves unlock. The last of minnows
like gray brushstrokes. We turn home
to see what's abandoned—

windowlight, Mason jars, blue corymbs of hydrangea,
fading like our skin that brushes past cicada husks,
snake skins, old burdens shucked. Death smells
like wood-smoke and clay, apple and ash,
thick as the slush our feet plume

near dank knuckles of water roots, mosquito eggs,
crane feathers trembling in shadows of bass.
Toads thrash the shore and plop into duckweed.
When we dive, the water sings away
the stories of our bodies,

our throats opened: grandmother's evening dress
drifts into the dark; grandfather opens his arms
in exaltation or dismay, all of us sinking below
circling gar and algal blooms
to where horse bones

shift in the slow pull, to the rich mud we take up
and eat, our mouths ripening,
white fire.

Strays

1.

Our bodies are wind passing through the wood.
We fear codices in the milkweed, blank as a cloud,

stems caught in frozen puddles. What good
are the trees to hide in, leafless, mere scrawls?

2.

We are orchard keepers, hidden in our roles,
rehearse the grove's momentum into apples.

Even our baskets are beautiful, heavy with their loads:
Now we wash our hair in the slick language of apples.

3.

The woods open our names and dissolve, lose context.
We grow old with the earth, years widening, concentric.

Will we make the weed-shrouded pond our currency,
lives spent forever beneath ordinary water, the warp

and flint of spring's light? No longer touchable,
we refuse the night's bone-cold alibi. Since our names

darken to char, our skin burns, turns to marl, will our bodies
become vessels of shadow, battened to the thrill of rain?

Hell

after Bosch

The damned might as well burrow into the earth,
let salt spill into wounds that reopen like blossoms,
red thrumming in the bone. They stumble

over slag-heaps, white-hot mud gasping at their feet,
cliffs sprung with emaciate grasses of human hair.
As sight dims, here, where they follow a skeletal light,

where the angel worm shimmers like a cloud as it hunts
to gnaw from them any memory of the earth, they reach
the parasite river, boats like wedges of rotten melon.

Water devours regenerate flesh, hauls them to caves
of forced resurrection, each new body trembling
with cumulative pain: they dig for all eternity

in the glare of gas flares, their hands soiled then burned
immaculate, again and again the radiance
of melting lungs the closest they will get to song.

The Tide

1.

She crosses the island to honor the dead.
Shells cut her feet, but she walks on,
throws a rock on his favorite shore.

Last night, she dreamed him by her side.
They walked inland among fronds and frogs
the color of terra cotta. She stopped to let rain

bloom in her hair. He placed his hand in a puddle
of stump-water, let his fingers glide through
billions of rotifers, paramecia's cilia.

2.

She wipes away the shells, rinses
feet in brine.

Behind gray windows,
the sting of ablution, of absence,
in this diminishing room.

So dying sea-grass shivers.
So curtains are drawn.

High tide: the east carves
a blue bowl of stars.

In Defiance of Autumn

1.

The wind, fall's perfect knife,
shucks the oaks' red pennants:
roof-slant and cell's pendulum, season
of downward fire.

Smells of resin, all sweetness
and tangibility, cease under
frost. The mountain's austere syllable.

2.

I know death
is the worm drowsing under the leaves,
coiling and uncoiling. I know the heart
gives way to char.

Behind this window,
on a chipped blue dish,
an overturned pear, a lantern that spills
oil of the sky's flame:

How precise,
stars silenced in the mottled flesh,
warm language of second sight.

Gravity

The scorched tree in a spring meadow,
its limbs a black calculus,
is not a lesson granted by the dead.

The dead do not walk brazenly, like an imam
striding the dawn of a Turkish city, sunlight
shedding gowns of milk. They do not prophesy

like hairline cracks in the plaster, stone ceilings
worn with rain, do not foretell
like deer's maggots lodged in deep grass,

in foxtail and thistle on field's edge. Still,
we catch a fragrance like rosemary, hear
pleas in murmurs of summer storm,

glimpse them in grackles scattering to shadow.
Why should we name them, these
gravities that lumber the heart?

At night's open door, we have stars in common,
those illusory souls, a sign that our words fill
the night's interstices with meaning,

that light darkened at its source for ten thousand years
still shimmers, memory's blue fire far outshining
the body long dimmed.

Winter Oaks

All night limbs hold
their blue lamplight aloft, ice
alive in the static understory.
I know how winter pulls the body

northward, makes the heart a cellar
in a sleepless house.
I know grass shatters
under that ossified eye. And just now,

when something moves in the mind
like a bluebird caught in an attic,
panicked, erratic, or descends
like the season's first snowfall,

I walk out to the oaks, bulbs
of my lungs shocked by the cold.
The night says: *Your breath unlocks the air with flowers.*
The night says: *Don't seek an easier way.*

About the Author

William Wright is the author of four other poetry collections, two full-length works and two chapbooks. His full-length collections are *Dark Orchard*, winner of the 2005 Breakthrough Poetry Prize (Texas Review Press, 2005) and *Bledsoe* (Texas Review Press, 2011); his chapbooks include *The Ghost Narratives*, published by Finishing Line Press in 2008 and *Sleep Paralysis*, which recently won the South Carolina Poetry Initiative Prize and is scheduled to be published soon. Wright's poetry has recently been published in *Shenandoah*, *North American Review*, *AGNI*, *Colorado Review*, *Indiana Review*, *Louisiana Literature*, *Beloit Poetry Journal*, *Southern Poetry Review*, and *Texas Review*, among other literary journals. Wright is series editor and volume co-editor of the ongoing *Southern Poetry Anthology*. The third and most recently published volume, focused on contemporary Appalachian poets, was released in 2010 by Texas Review Press.